S0-ACT-552

EYE to EYE with ANIMALS

STEALTHY SHARKS

by Ruth Owen

WINDMILL BOOKS

New York

Published in 2013 by Windmill Books, An Imprint of Rosen Publishing
29 East 21st Street, New York, NY 10010

Copyright © 2013 by Windmill Books, An Imprint of Rosen Publishing

All rights reserved. No part of this book may be reproduced in any form without permission in writing from the publisher, except by a reviewer.

Produced for Windmill by Ruby Tuesday Books Ltd
Editor for Ruby Tuesday Books Ltd: Mark J. Sachner
US Editor: Sara Antill
Designer: Emma Randall

Photo Credits:
Cover, 1, 7, 11, 15, 27, 28–29 © FLPA; 4–5, 17, 19, 20–21 © Shutterstock; 8, 23, 24–25 © Superstock; 9 © Terry Goss, Creative Commons, Wikipedia; 12–13 © Albert Kok, Creative Commons, Wikipedia; 16 © Nature Picture Library.

Library of Congress Cataloging-in-Publication Data

Owen, Ruth, 1967–
  Stealthy sharks / by Ruth Owen.
      p. cm. — (Eye to eye with animals)
  Includes index.
  ISBN 978-1-4488-8072-0 (library binding) — ISBN 978-1-4488-8108-6 (pbk.) —
ISBN 978-1-4488-8114-7 (6-pack)
  1. Sharks—Juvenile literature. I. Title.
  QL638.9.O94 2013
  597.3—dc23
                                        2012009790

Manufactured in the United States of America

CPSIA Compliance Information: Batch # B2S12WM: For Further Information contact Windmill Books, New York, New York at 1-866-478-0556

CONTENTS

Meet the Sharks!

They live in the ocean, have powerful, streamlined bodies, and huge numbers of teeth, and many are top predators. Meet the sharks!

Sharks have been on Earth for around 400 million years. As carnivorous dinosaurs stalked their **prey** on land, sharks hunted in our planet's prehistoric seas. The dinosaurs are long gone, but sharks, the biggest members of the **fish** family, still live in the Earth's oceans.

In movies, sharks delight and terrify us. Today, however, sharks have far more to fear from us than we do from them. Every year, 100 million sharks are killed by humans for their meat and fins, and many shark **species** are now seriously **endangered**.

So let's go eye to eye with some of the world's largest creatures and most magnificent predators, and find out how they live and what the future holds for them.

Fin

A scuba diver photographs a tiger shark.

A great white shark

THE BIGGEST DANGER TO SHARKS

Around 73 million sharks are killed each year so that their fins can be used to make shark fin soup. The sharks are often thrown back into the water, still alive, after their fins have been cut off. Shark fin soup is a popular dish in China and other parts of Asia.

GREAT WHITE SHARKS
Top Predator

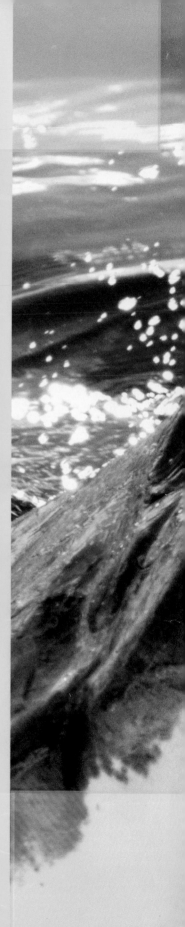

Body length: 14 to 18 feet (4.3–5.5 m)

Weight: 1,500 to 4,000 pounds (680–1,800 kg)

Description: Large, powerful, streamlined body; gray skin on top half of body and white belly

Lifespan: 30 years

Breeding age (females): 14 to 16 years

Breeding age (males): 9 to 10 years

Diet: Seals, elephant seals, sea lions, dolphins, turtles, sea birds

Key fact: Great white sharks are the largest predatory shark.

FACE FACTS

A great white shark's mouth can open nearly 4 feet (1.2 m) wide! When attacking prey, the shark's bottom teeth hold the prey in place, while the top teeth tear into the flesh.

Great white shark

7

Great white sharks have a scary reputation thanks to movies, such as *Jaws*, but they rarely attack humans.

Top Hunters

There have only been around 300 great white shark attacks on humans since people began keeping records. Most scientists believe that these attacks happen when great whites mistake a swimmer or surfer for a seal or sea lion.

Great whites find their prey by picking up tiny electrical charges in the water made by another animal's heart or movements. They can also smell blood if an animal is injured. In fact, they can smell a drop of blood in 26 gallons (100 L) of water.

A great white leaps from the ocean during a hunting attack.

A great white shark

Baby Great Whites

Great white shark **pups** grow in eggs inside their mother's body. Then they hatch inside her body and are born ready to swim away and start hunting. A female great white gives birth to up to 10 pups at one time. Each pup is around 4 feet (1.2 m) long.

HUNTING SKILLS

Great white sharks often position themselves below their prey. Then they attack fast from underneath. Some sharks have been seen bursting out of the water with their prey in their mouths.

Great White Sharks In Danger

Like many shark species, great whites are in danger from hunting.

Because of their ferocious reputation, people want to catch and kill them for sport.

They are killed for their fins to be used as food. Their giant jawbones can be sold for thousands of dollars to people who want a great white souvenir.

Large fishing boats often catch them accidentally in fishing nets.

GREAT WHITE SHARK RANGE MAP

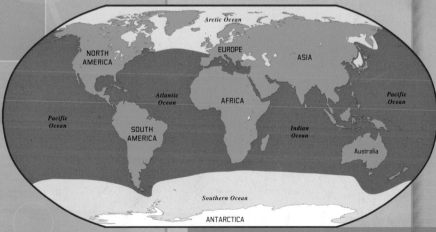

The red areas on the map show where great white sharks live.

9

TIGER SHARKS
Nighttime Hunters

Body length: 10.5 to 24 feet (3.2–7.3 m)

Weight: 840 to 1,900 pounds (381–862 kg)

Description: Blue or green-colored body with a white or light yellow belly

Lifespan: 27 years

Breeding age (females): 8 years

Breeding age (males): 7 years

Diet: Dead or injured whales, dugongs, stingrays, sea turtles, sea snakes, sea birds, octopuses, squid, and shellfish

Key fact: Tiger sharks try many different foods. They've even been found with tires in their stomachs!

FACE FACTS

Tiger sharks have serrated teeth that look like the edges of a saw. These teeth easily tear through flesh and can crunch through the shells of sea turtles.

Adult tiger shark

Adult tiger sharks usually hunt alone at night. They may swim up to 10 miles (16 km) in a 24-hour period looking for prey.

Surprise Attack

A tiger shark's color is good **camouflage** in water. This allows the shark to get close to prey without being seen. Then it strikes fast before its prey realizes the shark is there.

Little Hunters

Tiger shark pups grow in eggs inside their mother's body. Then they hatch inside her, and are born ready to swim away and hunt. A female tiger shark gives birth to up to 80 pups at one time. She does not take care of the pups or protect them from predators, such as adult sharks.

A remora fish swimming alongside a tiger shark

Tiger shark pups avoid predators by swimming fast. They also have stripes, which help to camouflage them in rippled water. Many tiger shark pups, however, do not survive to become adults. The tiger shark gets its name from the stripes on the pups' bodies.

A young tiger shark

WHERE YOU GO, I GO

Tiger sharks often have small fish called remoras, or sharksuckers, living with them. A remora attaches itself to the shark using a sucker-like body part. It uses the shark as a way to get around. It also gets to feed on the shark's leftovers.

Tiger Sharks In Danger

No one knows how many tiger sharks are living in the world's oceans.

Tiger sharks are caught in large numbers for their fins and meat, and for their livers, which are used to make a vitamin oil.

It's hard for tiger shark numbers to build because females only have young every three years. Many of the pups that are born are eaten by predators and do not grow into adults.

TIGER SHARK RANGE MAP

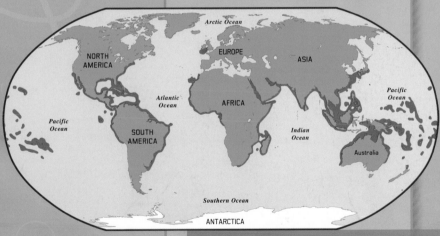

The red areas on the map show where tiger sharks live wild.

HAMMERHEAD SHARKS
A Head for Hunting

Body length: 13 to 20 feet (4–6 m)

Weight: 500 to 1,000 pounds (230–450 kg)

Description: Gray-brown to olive-green bodies with white bellies

Lifespan: Up to 30 years

Diet: Stingrays, smaller sharks, fish, octopuses, squid, lobsters, and crabs

Key fact: There are nine different species of hammerhead sharks. The largest is the great hammerhead.

FACE FACTS

A hammerhead shark gets its name from the shape of its head, which looks like the head of a hammer. The shark's eyes are on either end of its hammerlike head.

A hammerhead shark is an active, aggressive hunter.
The unusual shape of its head helps it find prey.

Detecting Prey

The hammerhead shark's wide-apart eyes allow it to better scan
the ocean looking for prey. Also, the organs in its head that pick
up electrical charges from prey are spread over the large head.
This gives the shark more chances of detecting prey.
A hammerhead shark can even detect stingrays, its favorite
food, when they are buried in sand on the seabed.

Hammerhead Pups

A female hammerhead shark gives birth to a **litter** of around six to
40 pups at one time. The pups are able to swim and take care of
themselves as soon as they are born.

The largest species of hammerhead shark
is the great hammerhead shark.
The pups of this species are
about 25 inches (65 cm)
long when they
are born.

Great hammerhead shark

A school, or group, of scalloped hammerhead sharks

Hammerhead Sharks In Danger

All hammerhead shark species are under threat from too much fishing.

Hammerhead sharks are caught for their fins for shark fin soup.

Sometimes hammerheads are killed when they are caught accidentally in fishing nets.

HAMMERHEAD SHARK RANGE MAP

Arctic Ocean

NORTH AMERICA

EUROPE

ASIA

Atlantic Ocean

AFRICA

Pacific Ocean

Pacific Ocean

SOUTH AMERICA

Indian Ocean

Australia

Southern Ocean

ANTARCTICA

The red areas on the map show where hammerhead sharks live wild.

HAMMERHEAD MIGRATION

Adult hammerhead sharks usually live alone. Sometimes, during warm months, scalloped hammerheads come together in **schools**, or groups, to **migrate**. They move from the warm oceans where they usually live to cooler waters.

17

WHALE SHARKS
The Largest Shark

Body length: Up to 66 feet (20 m)

Weight: Up to 37 tons (34 t)

Description: Upper body is gray-blue with white spots and a checkerboard pattern

Lifespan: 60 to 100 years

Breeding age (females): Approximately 30 years

Breeding age (males): Approximately 30 years

Diet: Plankton (microscopic animals and plants), and tiny fish, shellfish, and squid

Key fact: Whale sharks are the biggest fish in the world.

FACE FACTS

A whale shark's enormous mouth can be 5 feet (1.5 m) wide. The mouth contains thousands of tiny teeth arranged in 300 rows. The teeth aren't used for feeding, though.

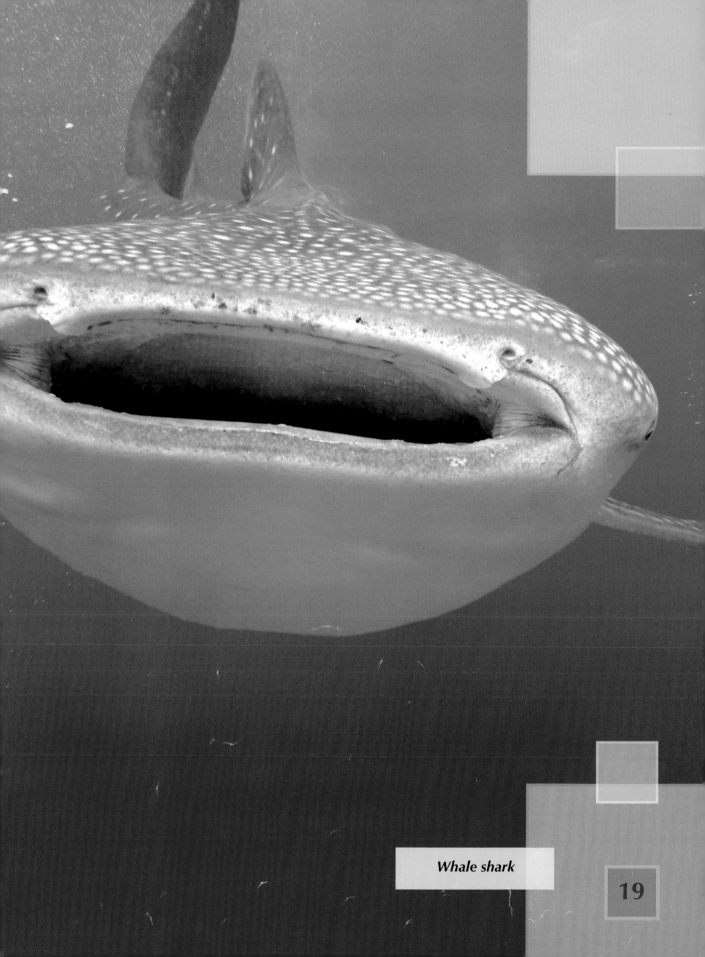

Whale shark

19

Whale sharks swim very slowly, traveling less than 1 mile per hour (1.6 km/h).

Slow-Moving Filter Feeders

Whale sharks may move slowly, but they make extremely long journeys. One whale shark, which was tracked by scientists for three years, traveled 8,000 miles (13,000 km) in that time.

These giant sharks are filter feeders. Their huge mouths suck in around 400,000 gallons (1.5 million L) of water an hour. The water is then passed out through the shark's **gills**. Sievelike structures in the gills filter, or trap, microscopic plankton and tiny animals, which the shark then eats.

A whale shark comes mouth to face with a scuba diver. These gentle, ocean giants are not dangerous to humans.

DEEP SEA DIVERS

Whale sharks sometimes dive to great depths. One shark that was being studied by scientists dived to 3,200 feet (980 m)!

Whale Shark Pups

Whale shark pups grow inside eggs and emerge from the eggs while inside their mother. Then the mother shark gives birth to the pups. The baby whale sharks can measure up to 25 inches (64 cm) when they are born.

Whale Sharks In Danger

Whale sharks are threatened by fishing and damage to their ocean habitat.

Whale sharks are hunted for their fins and meat.

Oil, chemicals, and pollution from boats damage ocean habitats. Pollution can harm the whales and destroy the plankton they feed on.

Whale sharks feeding at the water's surface are sometimes hit by boats.

WHALE SHARK RANGE MAP

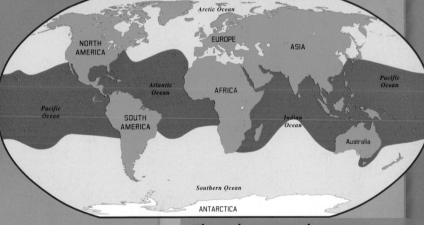

The red areas on the map show where whale sharks live wild.

21

BASKING SHARKS
Big Mouth!

Body length: Up to 33 feet (10 m)

Weight: Up to 7.7 tons (7 t)

Description: Gray-brown bodies with five huge gill slits on either side of the head.

Lifespan: 32 years

Breeding age (females): 12 to 16 years

Breeding age (males): 12 to 16 years

Diet: Plankton (microscopic animals and plants

Key fact: Second largest fish in the world.

FACE FACTS

Basking sharks swim with their giant mouths wide open. Their huge gill slits can easily be seen.

Basking shark

23

Basking sharks sometimes feed and travel alone. They are also seen in schools of hundreds of sharks feeding together.

Basking Shark Lives

Basking sharks swim for very long distances finding and feeding on plankton. One shark, which was tracked by scientists, crossed the Atlantic Ocean. It swam from the United Kingdom to Newfoundland, Canada, sometimes diving up to 0.75 miles (1.2 km) below the ocean.

A basking shark feeds by swimming with its mouth open. Water floods into the shark's mouth and out through its gills. The gills have long, comblike structures called gill rakers that trap the plankton in the water the shark has sucked in. The shark then swallows this food.

Basking Shark Pups

Scientists know very little about basking shark reproduction and young. One thing they do know, however, is that baby basking sharks are big! A newborn basking shark pup can measure up to 6.5 feet (2 m) long.

Basking shark

24

This view from behind a basking shark clearly shows its gill slits.

Basking Sharks In Danger

Basking sharks are under threat because they've been hunted in large numbers in the past.

Basking sharks were caught for their livers, fins, and meat.

About one quarter of a basking shark's weight is its huge liver. The oil from sharks' livers is used to make an oil that many people believe is good for human health.

It is now against the law to catch basking sharks.

BASKING SHARK RANGE MAP

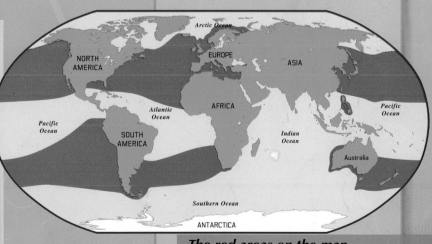

The red areas on the map show where basking sharks live wild.

SHARK SHOW-OFFS

Basking sharks sometimes leap completely out of the water and then crash back down. This is called breaching. Some scientists think that breaching could be linked to **mating**. A shark might be showing a potential mate how healthy it is!

25

GRAY NURSE SHARKS
A Toothy Grin

Body length: 12 feet (3.6 m)

Weight: 210 to 240 pounds (95–109 kg)

Description: Upper body is gray-brown with metallic, reddish brown spots, belly is white.

Lifespan: Up to 35 years

Breeding age (females): 7 to 8 years

Breeding age (males): 7 to 8 years

Diet: Small sharks, rays, fish, squid, lobsters, crabs

Key fact: Also known as the sand tiger shark and spotted ragged-tooth shark

FACE FACTS

The gray nurse shark has long, razor-like teeth, which can be seen even when the shark's mouth is closed. The shark constantly loses and grows teeth. In fact, each tooth is replaced about once every two weeks!

Gray nurse shark

This shark's fierce-looking, toothy grin earned it a reputation as a dangerous shark. Gray nurse sharks do not attack people, though.

Night Hunters

Gray nurse sharks live in warm, shallow waters, in bays, and close to **coral reefs**. They hunt at night and often spend the day in caves or close to rocky cliffs.

Tiny, Terrible Teeth

Gray nurse shark pups develop in eggs inside their mother. Then they hatch from their eggs and continue to grow inside their mother's body. Gray nurse shark pups grow teeth when they are just 2 inches (5 cm) long. Once their teeth have grown in, the developed pups may eat their undeveloped brothers and sisters before they are even born!

A female gray nurse shark usually gives birth to two fully developed pups at one time. The newborn pups can measure up to 5 feet (1.5 m) long. As soon as they are born, they are ready to take care of themselves.

SHARK TEAMWORK

Sometimes gray nurse sharks hunt as a team. They chase and herd fish, forcing them to gather in a group. Then the sharks can dive into the group to get a meal.

Gray nurse shark

Endangered Gray Nurse Sharks

Gray nurse sharks were the first shark species to be protected by law. It is against the law to kill them.

Because gray nurse sharks look fierce, people mistakenly thought they were dangerous. This led to them becoming a target for hunters, and they were killed in large numbers.

It will take a long time for this shark's numbers to increase, because females only give birth to two pups at a time. Many pups are eaten by bigger sharks before they become adults.

GRAY NURSE SHARK RANGE MAP

The red areas on the map show where gray nurse sharks live wild.

GLOSSARY

aggressive (uh-GREH-siv)
Ready or likely to attack.

camouflage (KA-muh-flahj)
Hiding or blending into one's
background. A shark's skin
color or pattern can camouflage
it against its background.

coral reefs (KOR-ul REEF)
Underwater masses of hard,
rocklike matter made from the
skeletons of tiny sea animals,
called corals, that are joined
together. When a coral dies, its
skeleton remains, so the mass
of coral grows larger and larger.

endangered (in-DAYN-jerd)
In danger of no longer existing.

fish (FISH)
Cold-blooded animals that live
in water. Fish breathe through
gills and have a skeleton, and
most lay eggs.

gills (GILZ)
Body parts that an underwater
animal uses for breathing.
The gills take oxygen out
of water and send it into the
animal's body.

litter (LIH-ter)
A group of baby animals all
born to the same mother at the
same time.

mating (MAYT-ing)
Coming together to produce
young.

migrate (MY-grayt)
To travel from one place to
another, often for one season,
in order to breed, find food, or
avoid hot or cold weather.

plankton (PLANK-ten)
Microscopic animals
and plants.

predator (PREH-duh-ter)
An animal that hunts and kills other animals for food.

prey (PRAY)
An animal that is hunted by another animal as food.

pups (PUPS)
The babies of sharks.

reputation (reh-pyoo-TAY-shun)
A widely held belief about someone or something, often based on a particular kind of behavior. Many sharks have a reputation for being dangerous to humans.

schools (SKOOLZ)
Large groups of fish.

species (SPEE-sheez)
One type of living thing. The members of a species look alike and can produce young together.

streamlined (STREEM-lynd)
Shaped and built in a way that helps something move more quickly through the air or water; often pointed and smooth.

Websites

For web resources related to the subject of this book, go to: www.windmillbooks.com/weblinks and select this book's title.

READ MORE

Musgrave, Ruth. *Everything Sharks: All the Shark Facts, Photos, and Fun That You Can Sink Your Teeth Into!*. Des Moines, IA: National Geographic Children's Books, 2011.

Nuzzolo, Deborah. *Tiger Shark*. Shark Zone. Mankato, MN: Capstone Press, 2011.

Randolph, Joanne. *The Hammerhead Shark: Coastal Killer*. Sharks: Hunters of the Deep. New York: PowerKids Press, 2007.

Roza, Greg. *Chomp!: The Great White Shark and Other Animals That Bite*. Armed and Dangerous. New York: PowerKids Press, 2011.

INDEX